# Business Credit Works

WHEN IT COMES TO BUILDING CREDIT,

THINK BUSINESS, NOT PERSONAL.

Darryl Johnson

Copyright:
Purpose Publishing
13194 U.S. 301 S. Suite #417
Riverview, FL 33578
www.PurposePublishing.com

Business Credit Works
Copyright © 2023 by Darryl Johnson
ISBN: 9798849036274

All rights reserved. No part of this publication may be reproduced, distributed, or transmitted in any form or by any means, including photocopying, recording, or other electronic or mechanical methods, without the prior written permission of the publisher, except in the case of brief quotations embodied in critical reviews and certain other noncommercial uses permitted by copyright law.

For permission requests, write to the publisher, addressed "Attention: Permissions Coordinator," at the address above.

Bulk Ordering Information: Quantity sales. Exclusive discounts are available on quantity purchases by groups, churches, ministry associations, etc.

Printed in the United States of America.

## DEDICATION

This book is dedicated to small business owners across the world that needed help and got it. It is also dedicated to small business owners who do not know they need the help, and someone placed a tool in their hands. This is book is my gift, the tool, back to you all. Every small business owner who gets this I ask you to gift this to another. Each one, reach one. Each one, teach one. Each one, beseech one.

# PREFACE

Welcome to the Business Credit Works, the book.

This book was created to educate, empower, and provide options to business owners in their quest to own, build and expand their businesses. It is an imperative to have your business credit in place to do so and without hiccups. Before we get started, I must ask you a few questions.

How many of these questions, can you answer yes?

- ✓ Are you using personal credit to finance, grow, operate your business?
- ✓ Has your credit score dropped because you have maxed out your credit cards?
- ✓ Is your home now or in the past been in jeopardy of being repossessed because you have taken all the equity out to fund your business?
- ✓ Have you ever had to do a personal guarantee for funding or credit for your business?

If you answered yes to one or all the questions above, it is okay. Everyone here is because they either have a problem that needs to be solved or you are pro-active vs. reactive. Either way, you are in the right place. Here is what I say about you, the business owner for taking this step and jumping into this book.

- You know there is a better, smarter way to open, grow and expand your business.

- You are looking for options and seeking knowledge.
- When it comes to credit, you are now thinking in terms of business credit not personal credit.
- You know that business credit makes good financial sense.

We are now introducing the Business Credit Works Book that is a companion and resource to the Business Credit Online course. In both the book and course, we cover topics like:

- Learn how business scores work
- What SBA lenders look for to obtain SBA funding
- Why your name can get you denied for business credit
- List of Tier 1,2,3,4 Vendor accounts
- And much, much more

You can check out the online program by going to https://business-credit-works.newzenler.com/

The Business Credit Works Course has been featured on

Business Credit Works is backed by the Better Business Bureau and celebrates pride in business.

# TABLE OF CONTENTS

|  | Introduction |  |
|---|---|---|
| Chapter 1 | What is Business Credit? | 11 |
| Chapter 2 | Business Credit History | 17 |
| Chapter 3 | Business Credit – Public & Unprotected | 25 |
| Chapter 4 | Understanding How Business Credit Works | 29 |
| Chapter 5 | Your Business Credibility | 45 |
| Chapter 6 | How Business Credit Impacts Your Business | 49 |
| Chapter 7 | Business Credit Works Exclusive Program | 57 |
| About the Author | Darryl Johnson | 96 |

# INTRODUCTION

If you picked up this book, then you are ready to take an initiative-taking approach to setting your business up on a secure foundation. I am glad you are here. I am Darryl Johnson, entrepreneur, and business credit coach. Over the course of my thirty plus years of experience working for other people, moving into entrepreneurship, and now teaching and training others on business credit. I know the surefire ways to set up, structure and most importantly, secure my business enterprises and protect my personal interests. When I speak of personal interests, namely my family and my earnings. I can tell you assuredly that setting up business credit is by far one of the most important things you can do to mitigate any financial risks to your personal interests should your business experience a loss or closure which can happen very easily in a pandemic, economic downturn, during a health crisis or due to litigation against the business. You must protect yourself and establishing business credit is at the forefront of getting started.

I will not take long or even share some horrible story that taught me these lessons the hard way. I do not think it is necessary and more importantly. I want you to get the information you need out of this book to take immediate action in getting your business credit profile established right away. With that said, stay with the book until the end. You should be able to finish it within

1-2 settings of an hour and you will be well on your way to accomplishing your goal of securing the foundation of your business.

Enough said, let us get into the content. You are going to learn several things like:

- What is Business Credit, Benefits, and the Various Types of Credit?
- History of Business Credit and Personal Guarantees
- YOUR Credit and PUBLIC Knowledge
- Your Business Credit Scoring and Who Scores It
- The Credit Reporting Agencies (CRA)
- And much more

There will be no more myths, untruths or mystery surrounding business credit, how to acquire it and how to use it to strengthen your business. You will be armed and activated to get it done. So, let us get it started.

# CHAPTER ONE

## WHAT IS BUSINESS CREDIT?

**What is Business Credit?**

Business Credit is obtained in a Business's Name and Employer Identification Number or EIN for short. With business credit, the business builds its credit profile and credit score. With an established credit profile and score, the company will then qualify for credit. This credit is in the business name and based on the business's ability to pay, not the business owners. Since the company qualifies for the credit, in some cases, there is no personal guarantee.

Business credit is not hard to build, but it is a process. Once you know the proper steps to take and the right business credit vendors to get started. You are well on your way. Now, business credit building is not that much different than building consumer credit. You start with no credit established or no history. Next, get approval for new credit reports to the 'business' credit reporting agencies to develop an initial credit profile and score.

There are no federal, local, or state regulations for business credit protection, and a business can get denied, especially a new business. As well, you may never know why they were denied.

In the case of establishing personal credit, the process is the same except rather than using an EIN number. An individual uses their social security number which then becomes the foundation for personal credit. All debts, assets or liens and the like are attached to your personal score and based on satisfactory payment history and debt to income ratios determine an individual's credit score. While there are credit protection laws in place for personal credit. Often individuals find themselves in debt trouble or personal hardship when using their personal credit to secure their business. Therefore, I tell my clients to establish business credit and leave your personal credit separate. As you can see, there are significant differences in the two credit profiles and scores.

While keeping *personal and business expenses separate* will save time when you balance your books, there are many other surprising benefits to a business credit card.

If you own a small company or are a solopreneur, having a business credit card can make it easy for you to separate your personal and business expenses.

Not only can this save you time every month but having two separate statements can also make it *convenient for record-keeping and completing your annual tax return*. Some business credit cards will even offer online tools that can help you track your expenses — much more straightforward than saving a year's worth of invoices and receipts in a physical file!

Business credit cards typically offer a more extensive line of credit than your personal card, which means you can buy the things your business needs when you need them. If a critical piece of equipment breaks, you can fix or replace it without having to dip into your cash reserves.

The more data you have access to, the more informed decisions you can make about your spending patterns. A business credit card can help consolidate your monthly purchases, giving you a simple path to analyzing your spending.

Delegating buying to your employees not only allows you to focus on more strategic work it also empowers them to make necessary purchasing decisions without waiting for your sign-off.

Many business credit cards offer employee cards that link to your business' main account. You can easily monitor the purchases made on those cards, set spending limits, and receive alerts if an employee uses a card outside the merchant categories you have approved.

## The Benefits for Business Owners to Get a Business Credit Card

Now, let me start by sharing that there are multiple benefits of securing a business credit card. Access to cash and credit is every business's lifeline. Business credit allows a company to borrow money that can be used to purchase products or services. It is based on the trust that payment will be made in the future.

You may be asking, why establish business credit? For today's savvy and not-so-savvy business owners, having a separate legal entity, such as a corporation or limited liability company, provides the unique ability to create a credit identity with business credit reporting agencies, also known as a business credit profile.

A business credit profile is important because it is used by credit grantors to determine whether to extend credit to a business.

Before you establish business credit for the first time, the first step is to structure your business as a separate legal entity. Next, you will need to apply for a tax identification number, also known as an employer identification number. This is the number used to identify a business entity for tax filing and reporting purposes.

There are some business credit cards let you earn rewards on your purchases in the form of points, miles, or cashback. While points or miles may be beneficial for some business owners, choosing a card that earns rewards means you can turn around and use them toward business purchases.

Having a business credit card — and paying off the balance regularly — can help quickly boost your business credit rating, provided that the vendors and suppliers you work with report transactions to the credit bureaus. I direct my clients to specific resources for streamlining and simplifying this for you. When you know where to go to get what you need – business credit building becomes easy.

## PRACTICAL EXAMPLES OF BUSINESS CREDIT

### Bob's Lawns LLC – Smart Example

**Bob's Lawns Idea**
- Bob has an idea about starting a lawn service.
- He has experience cutting lawns with his neighbor in the summers after college.

**Bob establishes Business**
- Bob establishes a business entity as an LLC with the Secretary of State office
- Bob applies for an EIN
- Bob connects with Business Credit Works to establish his business credit

**Bob gets his business credit card**
- Bob purchases equiipment
- Bob aquires first 10 contracts for lawn service with customers
- Bob gets busy mowing lawns and bringing in cash
- No risk to his personal credit.

### Bart's Baking Company – Not So Smart Example

**Bart's Baking Idea**
- Bart has an idea about starting a baking company.
- He has good experience working in the bakery of his local grocery store and now wants to do it on his own.

**Bart gets started with zeal and energy**
- Bart gets started baking cakes and selling them at his church.
- He gets lots of orders and needs to rent a kitchen to cook in.
- The rent for the kitchen plus ingredients is getting expensive.

**Bart himself in a jam.**
- Bart has an order that he really wants to take on but he needs software to help him manage his order intake, invoices nd delivery.
- He maxed out his credit card to get the supplies for the order.

While these examples are oversimplified, the truth is still the truth. Bart using his personal funds and credit to manage his business is risky. It is easy to get into trouble when using personal funding to support your business. The better way is what Bob did and you should do too. Get started doing things right and you will be able to build and scale with no risk to our personal assets or business.

## CHAPTER 2

## BUSINESS CREDIT HISTORY

**Let us begin with a little history lesson on business credit.**

There are three major business credit bureaus, Experian, Equifax, and the original and oldest Dun and Bradstreet. Each of these companies has its unique history. We will talk about all these a little more in depth later in the book. But for now, let us look at the first establishment and continued name in the world of business credit, Dun & Bradstreet.

Dun & Bradstreet is the leading provider of business credit building and credibility solutions for businesses. We have chosen to focus and provide more information on Dun & Bradstreet since it is the oldest of the three and is used to get minority government contracts.

The company's roots can be traced back to the beginning of the credit industry when in 1837, the first credit information bureau was established in New York City by Mr. Church. The bureau was established to serve wholesalers who desired information concerning out-of-town merchants interested in commencing trade.

Dun & Bradstreet is the leading provider of credit building and credibility solutions for businesses. In the 1960s, Dun & Bradstreet expanded dramatically by engineering innovative ways to apply modern technologies to evolving operations.

Most notably, the introduction in 1962 of the Data Universal Numbering System – The D-U-N-S Number – helped standardize business information. This unique business identification system is used to catalog and organize businesses numerically for data processing purposes.

The D-U-N-S Number has become universally accepted as a standard business identifier for the United Nations, the European Commission, and the United States Government, among countless other government and business entities.

In 2001, Dun & Bradstreet Inc. changed its name to D&B, launching a new corporate brand with a powerful visual identity system. D&B is an institution, having spawned numerous companies and industries through its rich history.

Now, just so that we include them as part of the history conversation. There are other credit reporting agencies that you have heard of or have some knowledge. They are:

- Equifax is the second oldest of the three credit bureaus, dating back to 1899, when known as the Retail Credit Company.

- Experian is the newest of the credit bureaus. It was founded in 1996, making it a certified 90's kid.

- Transunion is the smallest of the three largest credit agencies.

Together, Equifax, Experian and TransUnion are considered THE BIG THREE in consumer credit reporting agencies although all three now offer services for both consumers and businesses. Dun & Bradstreet are still the major and premier agency for business credit reporting to date.

## The Differences Between Consumer & Business Credit

Having access to money and credit for your business determines your business's success or failure per the SBA. But per Entrepreneur.com, 90% of business owners know nothing about business credit. And ironically, about 90% of businesses in the United States that open end up failing and closing their doors for good. A good business credit profile and score can be the difference between having a prosperous business or being at the helm of a sinking ship.

You need money and credit to grow, especially to grow into a successful business. This is one commonality ALL successful businesses have: established business credit. Facebook, Microsoft, and every successful private and public company have business credit. The business can use its own credit profile to grow without the owner or CEO providing personal credit or liability to secure that credit. Walmart gets 80% of its total cash injection from business credit alone.

This is one of the reasons they have grown into one of the largest retailers in the world. But what about you? Do you have business credit established now? Can you go out right now and get a high-limit store and cash credit cards for your business? Can you do so without having to put your Social Security number on the application? If not, you need business credit. It may be the only thing holding you back from ultimate success.

We hear a lot about consumer credit in the news: "Consumer Credit is Up," "Consumer Credit is Flat," and so on. But what *is* the difference between consumer credit and business credit? And why you should care and how you are putting your family at risk of not establishing and separating the two credit profiles.

In general terms, consumer credit is debt taken on by individuals who intend to spend the funds right away. Business credit is debt taken on by the business.

**Types of Business Credit**

Once your business has been properly formed and in operation, the next step is to apply for credit in your company's name. There are several basic types of business credit you can acquire as a newly formed startup or existing business with little to no credit identity established.

- **Vendor Credit** – Vendor credit is when an individual or business offers products or services that your company can purchase on short term financing (typically net 30 terms). There are many vendors willing to extend credit to startups with minimal requirements. In some cases, a

vendor may require an initial purchase or deposit prior to extending credit terms.
- **Supplier Credit** – This type of business credit is when a supplier is willing to provide supplies to your business and defer the payment for a later date. This type of financing is great for conserving cash flow because it gives you time to sell the products you receive from the supplier before having to pay for them.
- **Retail Credit** – Many small and major brand retailers offer store credit cards for businesses. Unless they are co-branded, the card can only be used in a specific store. This type of business credit may make sense if you have a specific store, you regularly use for business purchases.
- **Service Credit** – The easiest form of business credit you can establish for the first time is service credit. Your internet, cell phone, cable, satellite TV, web hosting and other utility services are all agreements your company makes with providers.
- **Business Credit Cards** – One of the most important tools to keep your personal and business purchases separate is a secured or unsecured business credit card. It is essential that you apply for a business credit card that reports only to the business credit agencies so you can protect your personal credit as well.

These are five ways you can establish credit for your business for the first time. It is important to closely monitor your business credit reports and scores on a regular basis to ensure the information reporting is accurate and up to date.

Remember, by establishing business credit; banks, lenders, suppliers, retailers, insurers & investors will now be able to better access the viability and creditworthiness of your business. Ultimately, your business credit report will impact the amount of credit, payment terms, interest rates and insurance premiums your business will pay.

**What is a Personal Guarantee?**

When you put your SSN on a credit application, you are always providing a personal guarantee. This means you are personally liable for your business debts, so if you default on an obligation, the creditor will pursue your business assets first. Then they will come after your assets. These include your home, cars, stocks and bonds, bank accounts, and other assets.

Business owners do not expect to fail. But unfortunately, 90% do. It makes no sense to put you and your family's financial future in jeopardy. Do not do this when you know going in that you have a 90% possibility of ruining it.

Remember, many times, the reasons a business might fail have nothing to do with you or things you can control. This can include shifts in the economy. So do not risk it all if you do not have to.

There is no question, starting and running a business is risky. Therefore, most conventional banks make it so hard to get a loan. So do not use a personal guarantee unless you must. With many business loans, you must. But with the credit, you do not need to if you build business credit.

A personal guarantee is an agreement that makes one liable for one's own or a third party's debts or obligations. A personal guarantee signifies that the lender (oblige) can lay claim to the guarantor's assets in case of the borrower's (obligor's) default. It is like a signed blank check without a date. The oblige is not made to seek repayment first from the obligor's assets before going after the guarantor's assets.

The lender's actions are usually based on whose assets are easier to take control of and sell. Once signed, the oblige can only cancel a personal guarantee. They are also sometimes necessary for larger loan amounts. They are always requested for loans guaranteed by the SBA and conventional bank loans. And it is also required with some other higher loan amounts with no pledged collateral. When you complete a loan application and provide your SSN, lenders always pull your credit to decide on lending. Often, you are providing a personal guarantee.

# PRACTICAL EXAMPLES OF CREDIT TYPES

## Bob's Lawns LLC – Smart Example

**Bob's Lawns Idea**
- Bob has an idea about starting a lawn service.
- He has experience cutting lawns with his neighbor in the summers after college.

**Bob establishes Business**
- Bob establishes a business entity as an LLC with the Secretary of State office
- Bob applies for an EIN
- Bob connects with Business Credit Works to establish his business credit

**Bob gets his business credit card**
- Bob purchases equiipment
- Bob aquires first 10 contracts for lawn service with customers
- Bob gets busy mowing lawns and bringing in cash
- No risk to his personal credit.

## Bart's Baking Company – Not So Smart Example

**Bart's Baking Idea**
- Bart has an idea about starting a baking company.
- He has good experience working in the bakery of his local grocery store and now wants to do it on his own.

**Bart gets started with zeal and energy**
- Bart gets started baking cakes and selling them at his church.
- He gets lots of orders and needs to rent a kitchen to cook in.
- The rent for the kitchen plus ingredients is getting expensive.

**Bart himself in a jam.**
- Bart has an order that he really wants to take on but he needs software to help him manage his order intake, invoices nd delivery.
- He maxed out his credit card to get the supplies for the order.

## CHAPTER 3

## BUSINESS CREDIT IS UNPROTECTED & PUBLIC INFORMATION

**Did you know that anyone Can Pull your Business Credit?**

Business credit is public information. This means anyone who seeks your business can get it, quickly and cheaply. Consider this, people can review your reports whenever they want. These people could be customers, clients, suppliers, contractors, lenders, and even your competitors.

Here is a quick list of information that anyone can see about your business:

- Number of tradelines (payment experiences)
- Credit scores
- High credit limits
- Past payment performance
- Number of Employees
- Revenues

And even more is available to anyone who seeks it.

Now, what does your profile say about you? Are you established? Would you want to do business with a company with a similar profile? How will your customers, clients, even competitors think about you with this information?

It is important to monitor your reports regularly to see what others can know about you. You want to keep building your business credit. Then, you will be able to show a credible image to anyone who wants to see your credit in the future. This is for those who lend money or issue credit.

Another important fact that you may not know.

**Business Information Is Public Knowledge!**

- Businesses use credit scores to extend credit to other businesses. Creditors and vendors are under no obligation to tell you which scores they are relying upon.

- Competitors, **clients**, and business prospects can also review your report. Most creditors use LexisNexis report for legal, regulatory, business information, and risk management services. It is used to assess risk on applicants.

- Inaccurate information or negative items in this report can have a drastic negative impact on your business. This is especially true during the application process.

**No Right to Privacy**

Anyone can review your business credit reports for any reason. There is no right to privacy when it comes to corporate credit reports. The business credit bureaus can sell your credit information to anyone they wish.

This is one more reason working to establish and maintain strong business credit is an important responsibility to add to your to-do list.

# CHAPTER 4

# UNDERSTANDING HOW BUSINESS CREDIT WORKS

**How Business Credit Scores Works**

Many small business owners do not realize that business credit scores are distinctly separate from personal credit scores. Your business credit score has no impact on your credit score and vice versa. A business credit report shows the same types of information as a personal credit report. Still, it is specific to a business's debt repayment and public records, such as bankruptcies or tax liens.

Three leading business reporting agencies provide your business credit profile and score. They are *Dun & Bradstreet, Experian, and Equifax Commercial*. A business credit score is a mathematical model. It depicts a business's risk of going 90 days late on an account in the

Each reporting agency provides access to multiple business credit scores evaluating different forms of risk. FICO has its business credit score to assess business risk. Banks have their own internal bank credit score to determine business loan approvals. Credit issuers, lenders, suppliers, vendors, and others that extend credit to businesses use these scores.

Your business credit scores are used every time you apply for credit and financing for your business. But lenders and credit issuers will not tell you this. And they will not tell you which scores they use to assess your business. There is no Fair Credit Reporting Act in the business world requiring them to like there is in the consumer credit world

Business credit reflects your company's image to potential lenders and business partners. Yet, unlike personal credit -- which can be viewed only with the report holder's permission -- business credit scores are made available to the public. Anyone can view your business credit score for any reason.

**Your Business Credit Score Is Not Automatic**

Unlike consumer credit scoring, you must apply to get an EIN from the IRS website. Next, get a D-U-N-S number from Dun & Bradstreet (arrives in a few weeks).

Then tally up to three separate payment experiences. Then D&B starts tracking your business's financial activity, and you get a PAYDEX score.

**Business Credit Scoring System**

Furthermore, business credit is expressed with a different numerical range than personal credit. Business credit scores provide a quick view of a company's risk potential based on a scale of 1 to 100 -- the higher the score, the lower the risk.

The objective of the Business Credit Score to predict seriously derogatory payment behavior.

Your business credit profile and scores are available to anyone who wants them. In the consumer world, someone needs your permission to pull your consumer reports.

This is what the FCRA calls "permissible purpose." But with no FCRA in the business world, anyone who wants your reports can quickly and cheaply get them. This includes competitors, prospects, clients, lenders, and more.

| Business Credit Score Range | Risk Class | Risk Description |
|:---:|:---:|:---:|
| 76-100 | 1 | Low |
| 51-75 | 2 | Low to Medium |
| 26-50 | 3 | Medium |
| 11-25 | 4 | Medium to High |
| 1-10 | 5 | High |

## The Credit Reporting Agencies (CRA)

## Dun & Bradstreet Business Credit Scores

Dun & Bradstreet provides two Performance Credit Scores. These scores reflect a company's past performance using only information in the D&B database. D&B's two core Performance Scores are PAYDEX Score and D&B Rating z The PAYDEX Score – Shows how a company has paid its bills over the last 24 months z The D&B Rating – Indicates a company's net worth range based on company financial statements. It also shows a company's overall condition The most popular credit score used in the business world is the PAYDEX score from Dun and Bradstreet.

From D&B: "The D&B PAYDEX® Score is D&B's unique dollar-weighted numerical indicator of how a firm paid its bills over the past year, based on trade experiences reported to D&B by various vendors." "Dollar-weighted" means D&B gives more weight to accounts with higher limits than ones with lower limits. PAYDEX gives more weight to trade accounts reporting higher amounts of credit extended. And it gives less weight to trade accounts reporting lower dollar amounts of credit.

Any score of 70 and higher D&B defines as a good score. An 80 score reflects prompt payment. A score of 70 reflects payments are paid within 15 days of terms. Scores 50 or lower represent payments being made 30 or more days past terms. A business can get a good business PAYDEX credit score by ensuring payments are made promptly to suppliers and vendors.

A business needs a PAYDEX score of 70 – 80 for the most favorable financing. To get a PAYDEX score, a company needs at least three trade accounts reporting to their file. It can take 30 – 90 days for those trades to report and a score to be established.

**PAYDEX Scores**: are based on Payment History.

**Experian's Business Credit Scores:** The second most popular credit score in the business world is the Experian Intelliscore. Experian's most recent score system is Intelliscore Plus. They boast of it as the next level in credit scoring. Intelliscore Plus considers hundreds of variables to offer a business score between 0 – 100. Intelliscore predicts a business's risk of going seriously delinquent or over 91 days late. Or they were having a significant financial issue like bankruptcy in the next 12 months.

The new Intelliscore Plus has over 800 aggregates or factors affecting the score. Experian looks at business data segments like firmographics, public records, collections, and trade information. It then places each business in one of three different models.

Intelliscore is one of the only business scores offering a combined score. The Blended/ Owner Model blends commercial data and the owner's consumer information. Because this score blends with consumer data, it is one of the only scores where someone needs your permission to pull.

**Equifax's Business Credit Scores** Equifax's primary business credit scoring model is the Credit Risk Score. Equifax created this score to predict the probability of a business customer becoming seriously delinquent. A lower score indicates a higher risk of serious delinquency (90 days late) in 12 months. Credit scores range from 1 – 100. Like the D&B PAYDEX score, the Credit Risk Score comes from payment history. All that is necessary for a good score is to pay business obligations as agreed. The earlier payments are made, the higher the score is.

Equifax's Credit Risk Score:

| | |
|---|---|
| Paid as Agreed | 90 + |
| 1 – 30 days overdue | 80 – 89 |
| 31 – 60 days overdue | 60 – 79 |
| 61 – 90 days overdue | 40 – 59 |
| 91 – 120 days overdue | 20 – 39 |
| 120+ overdue | 1 – 19 |

The Business Failure Score predicts the likelihood of a business failure through formal or informal bankruptcy over the next 12 months. The Payment Index provides a dollar-weighted index of a business's current and past payment performance.

It is based on all payment experiences in the Equifax Commercial database. Equifax also offers a Business Failure Risk Score with many reports.

This score predicts the likelihood the business will fail or file for bankruptcy in the next 12 months. This model helps identify businesses that pose a greater risk for failure. This way, suppliers and credit grantors can take appropriate actions.

**The FICO SBSS score** is a measure of your small business's creditworthiness. This score is becoming extremely popular with lenders. This score has also become widely used to qualify business loans.

It comes from both personal and business credit history. he SBSS was launched in 1993 when the SBA started using it to evaluate all 7 (a) loans under $350,000.

SBSS scores range from 0 – 300. Higher scores are better and mean lower risk. Personal and business credit history, plus financial data, figure into the total score.

All SBA 7(a) loans must go through a business credit score prescreen. For SBA loans, you will not get approval with a score below 140. But they often set the cutoff as high as 160.

Below that, you will get a denial because of being too high a risk. And chances are good the SBA lender will not even submit your application to the SBA if your score does not meet this threshold.

If you have no business credit history and limited time in business, the highest possible FICO SBSS score you can get is 140. But to get a score as high as that, you must have pristine personal credit if no business credit is established.

If you have no business credit history and limited time in business, the highest possible FICO SBSS score you can get is 140. But to get a score as high as that, you must have pristine personal credit if no business credit is established.

**Chex Systems**

Banks and credit unions use Chex Systems to verify personal and business deposit accounts, history of delinquent use of accounts, and more.

Inaccurate information on a report can have a drastic negative impact on your business.

This is especially when you try to establish banking products.

Take control of your company's fundability by requesting a copy of your LexisNexis & Chex Systems report today!!!

**Did you know there is a tool and full-service resource out there for helping small businesses with their financing?**

**NAV (www.nav.com)**

- A personalized marketplace experience, personalized data-driven financial solutions empower business owners to make savvy decisions about their business' financial health.

- Easy-to-read personal and business credit reports and monitoring all in one spot.

- Free to sign up

- Get access to both personal and business credit reports.

- They are also compatible with our program to increase your chances to establish and grow your business.

## High Level Overview of Business Credit

Learning how to build and manage your *personal credit* may also be important. Many small business owners find their personal credit history is also important, because lenders may review the business owner's personal credit before approving a new account.

However, before you decide to borrow money, calculate the costs associated with the loan and the impact on your business. Getting approved for a loan does not always mean you should accept it.

Remember, you will need to repay the money plus fees and interest.

If you are borrowing money without a clear plan for how it will improve your business, or how you will repay the loan, you might not want to take on the debt. Otherwise, you could wind up using most of your company's revenue to repay debt and you will not have money left over for yourself or to invest in the company's future.

On the other hand, if you think a loan can help your business make or save more money than you will pay in fees and interest, then the loan might be a promising idea.

**The benefits of business credit**
In the *Business Credit* section, you can find the five steps you can take to establish and build good business credit.

In short, you'll need to *legally create* a business entity, such as a corporation or limited liability company. Then, you will have to open accounts with companies that report your payment history (such as on-time, ahead of schedule or late bill payments) to the business credit bureaus. If you have a line of credit or credit card, only using a small portion of the money you are allowed to borrow and consistently paying it off could help your business credit.

Establishing a good business credit history could help your business:

- Qualify for higher loan amounts and lower interest rates when borrowing money
- Pay less for business insurance
- Receive better agreements with suppliers

If you do not build business credit, you may be able to use your personal credit to borrow money for your business. However, your personal savings and possessions may be at risk if you cannot afford to repay the money you borrow using your personal credit. Additionally, using your personal credit for your business could make it more difficult to qualify for a personal loan, such as when you want to buy a vehicle or home.

Whether you rely on your business's credit, your personal credit, or a mix of both, you might consider three ways to borrow money: a credit line, a loan, or a credit card.

**Business credit line**
Opening a credit line gives you the option to borrow money in the future. When you open a credit line, your account will have a credit limit, which is the most money you can borrow at one time.

For example, you might get approved for a credit line with a $5,000 limit. You can take out one or multiple loans until the total amount is $5,000. Generally, you only pay interest or fees on the amount you borrow, so borrowing as little as possible will help save you money.

Credit lines are revolving accounts, and you can repeatedly borrow from the account without reapplying.

For example, you could borrow $1,000 from your $5,000 credit line and the lender will transfer the money into your account. Then, you will repay the $1,000 plus interest. Once you do, you can borrow up to the full $5,000 again.

Or you might be able to take out another loan while you are still repaying the first as long as the combined loan amounts are below $5,000.

Opening a line of credit could help ease concerns about money. You will have some certainty that you can borrow money if you need to pay for an expense or invest in a new opportunity. However, shop different lenders before opening a credit line, otherwise you might pay more in fees and interest than you need to. For example, some (but not all) accounts have an annual fee, which you will need to pay even if you do not take out a loan.

**Business loan**
You need to order a shipment of supplies or want to buy a vehicle so you can make deliveries. If there is a single expense that you cannot afford in full, taking out a business loan could be a good option.

With a *business loan*, you'll receive the full amount you want to borrow immediately and will repay the money, plus interest, over time. There are some special types of business loans, such as equipment loans that you can use to buy (rather than rent) an expensive piece of equipment.

The amount of money you can borrow, interest you pay and how long you must repay the loan can depend on many factors, including:

- The lender
- Your personal credit
- Your business's credit
- Your business plan
- How much money your business makes
- How long you have been in business
- Whether you offer collateral, which is something of value the lender can take if you cannot repay the loan, such as a house, business building or vehicle.

Lenders may have different requirements and offers, and shopping around to get multiple loan offers could help you secure a good loan. Many small business owners may need to sign a personal guarantee for a business loan, meaning they agree to repay the loan if the business is not able to make its payments.

**Business credit card**
You can use a business credit card to pay for everyday business expenses, and in case you need to borrow money. Business credit cards may offer some benefits that are not available on personal credit cards, such as:

- Employee cards, which let you give an employee a credit card that is tied to your business account. You may be able to limit how much the employee can spend and where the employee can use the card.
- Using a business card could help separate your personal and business expenses, which will make it easier to keep accurate business records and organize your expenses before filing tax returns.
- A business credit card could help your business build its credit history.
- Purchases and balances on your business credit card might not impact your personal credit history. However, you may still be personally responsible for the debt, and unpaid business credit card accounts could wind up on your personal credit reports.

Credit cards tend to have higher interest rates than credit lines or loans, and they may be a more expensive form of financing for larger purchases if you are unable to pay them off right away. However, they can offer a good short-term solution for managing day-to-day expenses.

**Types of Credit**

Now, let us talk about Types of Credit that you can put into action right away for your small business. When establishing business credit, there are three types of credit you can get:

- Vendor credit, starter accounts that offer Net 30 terms.
- Retail credit, revolving credit cards available in retail stores.
- Cash credit, revolving credit cards like Visa and MasterCard. Card issuers or banks approve you for these.

**Vendor Credit** (Also known as a Trade Account)

The vendor or supplier becomes the lender by allowing customers to "buy now" and "pay later."

- The standard terms are Net 30, Net60, Net 90
- When applying for trade accounts, make sure: Your business information matches all your business records and makes a purchase of over $50.
- It typically takes 30-90 days for your payments to report on your business credit reports.
- Continue to search your reports regularly, so you are aware when they start reporting.

**Retail Credit Cards**

- Once you have five vendor accounts reporting to the business credit reporting agencies, next, you can start to secure revolving retail credit cards for your EIN.

- Some sources might have more stringent approval requirements, like Home Depot.

- Requiring significant revenue and three years in business for approval with no personal guaranteed credit.

- But most sources do not have these requirements if business credit is already established.

Did you know? There is a real risk to applying for a revolving retail credit without at least 3-5 payment experiences reporting. If you do, any of these adverse things can and will happen:

**(1) You will get denied.**

**(2) You will be asked for a personal guarantee or**

**(3) You will be started with a lower credit limit.**

However, this can be avoided. Keep reading.

**Cash Credit Cards**

- Cash cards are those issued by Visa, MasterCard, and even AMEX.

- Once you have a total of 10 or more payment experiences reported to the business credit bureaus, you can start to get cash credit cards.

These are the types of credit that can be used for building your business credit. Now, let us move into ensuring your business is ready for it.

# CHAPTER 5

## YOUR BUSINESS CREDIBILITY

Credibility in business is one of the key distinguishing characteristics between entrepreneurs who reach success and those who fade into obscurity. You may offer a better product, but if you are known to lack credibility, it will adversely impact your company's staying power. This is especially true today given the multitude of platforms where news goes viral in a flash. Let us be sure yours is intact.

### Business Name

Try to choose the most basic and generic name possible.

- Do not get pegged into just one industry.
- There are a lot of industries that fall into restricted lists.
- General consulting type names work best as nobody will deny you.

### Your Business Address

Ensure you use a real physical address.

- *No* PO Box or UPS address

A virtual office is an option for those who do not have a business address.

### Your Business Phone

- Do not use a personal home phone or cell phone. (Yes, lenders will know!)

- Do not even try applying for funding without a genuine business phone.

- You should have a toll-free number unless you only deal with local businesses like a pizza shop.

- Your Number must have a listing with 411.
    - Try www.listyourself.net

**Did you Know?** There is a reason your business needs to be listed in 411. So, what is the 411 on 411? I am so glad you asked.

Credit issuers, suppliers, and lenders view a **411 listing** as a strong sign of business credibility that's only obtained by an established business.

Most credit issuers and lending sources **look to see if your number is listed with 411** before they'll issue you initial credit, or even a loan.

You can't just go to 411 direct to get your number listed, it has to "organically" happen. This means 411 will eventually add your number to their directory once they see your business listed at places online such as Bing or Google.

There is a way to *shortcut the process* so you don't have to wait for 411 to list you. There are services like *List Yourself* who will setup your 411 listing for you. They do have a limited free option as well. Other services like Yext can also get you listed with 411 as well, they are more expensive but list you in more places than just 411.

Whichever option you choose, <u>make sure your phone number is listed with 411</u> so you don't run into obstacles when trying to get credit and loans for your business.

### Your Business Fax

- Ensure you also get set up with a toll-free number and make sure you get a fax number.

- This is particularly important to get approval for initial, starter business credit.

### Your Professional Website

- Your website must look good and describe your products and services.

### Your Professional Email

Set up your professional email address. Keep your business email address professional. Look at the examples below and the difference it can make in the impression you give a potential creditor or client. Choose our email address wisely.

Darryl.Boss.Man@gmail.com vs. Darryl@businesscreditworks.com

### Setting up Your Business Entity

**Register your company with the Secretary of State**

- Choose an entity like a corporation or LLC (Limited Liability Corporation).
- Series LLC
- Talk to your tax professional!!!

**An Employer Identification Number (EIN)**

- This is the corporate equivalent to a Social Security number.
- Use irs.gov link ONLY. No 3$^{rd}$ party providers.

Note: Other links will try to charge you. But your EIN is free. **Don't pay a company for it!**

**Did you Know?**

There is a cost to be the boss. Ignoring your business credit can cost you.

The reality is that businesses need money to fund new expansions and other significant expenditures. For the business owner, having a solid business credit profile means that their borrowing power will be more than DOUBLE what it would be if they did not have business credit.

# CHAPTER 6

# THE MAIN REPORTING AGENCIES AND YOUR BUSINESS

We will start with a bit of a recap of what we talked about in Chapter 3 with the business credit agencies. The 3 Main Reporting Agencies.

There is a ton of reporting agencies, but the **three leading reporting agencies** are:

- Dun & Bradstreet - just for businesses
- Experian -both consumer and business
- Equifax - both consumer and business

All agencies depict a business's risk of going 90 days late on an account in the next 12 months. In comparison, consumer scores represent risk over a 24-month period. Reflects the business's likelihood of defaulting on an obligation, not the business owners.

Each reporting agency provides access to multiple business credit scores evaluating different forms of risk.

**Dun & Bradstreet**

Provides Two Performance Credit Scores, Paydex score, and D&B Rating.

**PAYDEX Score**

- This score shows how a company has paid its bills over the last 24 months.

- Dollar-weighted" means D&B gives more weight to accounts with higher limits than ones with lower limits.
- The score ranges from 1 – 100 it can take 30 – 90 days for those trades to report and a score to be established

**D&B Rating**

- Indicates a company's net worth range based on company financial statements. It also shows a company's overall condition.
- The D&B Rating is broken into three distinct categories.
  - Category 1 – Traditional D&B Rating
  - Category 2 – Expanded Credit Appraisal
  - Category 3 – Alternative Ratings

**Experian**

- Intelliscore Plus considers hundreds of variables to offer a business score between 0 – 100.
- The purpose is to determine the business's risk of going seriously delinquent or over 91 days late and having a significant financial issue like bankruptcy in the next 12 months.
- The score is calculated based on multiple factors:
  - **Credit:** Number of trade experiences, balances outstanding payment habits, credit utilization, and trends over time.

- **Public Records:** Recency, frequency, and dollar amounts associated with liens, judgments, or bankruptcies.
- **Demographic Information:** Years on file, Standard Industrial Classification (SIC) code, and business size.

## Equifax

- Equifax created this score to predict the probability of a business customer becoming seriously delinquent.
- A lower score indicates a higher risk of serious delinquency (90 days late) in 12 months.
- Credit scores range from 1 – 100
- Credit Risk Score comes from payment history.
  - All that is necessary for a good score is to pay business obligations as agreed.
  - The earlier payments are made, the higher the score is.

Therefore, it costs to be the boss. Your business credit can make all the difference in how much and how worth your business is. And you now have the power in your hands to rightfully influence it for the better.

It is possible that you are already working with suppliers who are reporting or not reporting to the credit bureaus. It is time to find out which are, and which are not. What can you do if the suppliers you work with do not report to credit bureaus?

## Manually Reporting

If you are making on-time payments to a supplier who is not reporting your payments, you are not helping build your business credit history.

The truth is some suppliers are not reporting to credit bureaus. Simply asking if they are willing to do this might be all you need to get them to report.

### Step 1 – Reach out to your suppliers

Check if they are willing to report; let them know it will not cost anything.

- If this does not work, tell them you are willing to find another vendor/supplier.

**NOTE:** If you say that, be willing to walk away.

### Step 2 – Provide Supplier Request Form

Some vendors/suppliers might not be large enough to qualify for reporting to bureaus. But if they are large enough, you can help them get started by downloading this supplier request template.

Remember....Simply asking if they are willing to do this might be all you need to get them to report.

### What's Driving Your Credit Score?

Many people do not know what makes up one's consumer credit score. Here is the short answer and we will dive into it a little further in the next few pages. Your Payment history, debt-to-credit ratio, length of credit history, new credit, and the amount of credit you have all play a role in your credit report and credit score.

So, what impacts it the most? I am glad you asked, and I want to share with you my concise list of the 5 Biggest Issues That Impact Consumer Credit Score & Why.

## 5 Biggest Issues That Impact Consumer Credit Score

### 1. Payment History: 35%

One key question lenders have on their minds when they give someone money: "Will I get it back?"

Your credit score's most critical component looks at whether you can be trusted to repay funds loaned to you. This component of your score considers the following factors:

- Have you paid your bills on time for each account on your <u>credit report</u>? Paying late hurts your score.
- If you have paid late, how late were you—30 days, 60 days, or 90+ days? The later you are, the worse it is for your score.

### 2. Amounts Owed: 30%

So, you might make all your payments on time, but what if you are about to reach a breaking point?

<u>FICO</u> scoring considers your <u>credit utilization ratio</u>, which measures how much debt you have compared to your available credit limits. This second-most vital component looks at the following factors:

- How much of your total <u>available credit</u> have you used? Do not assume you have to have a $0 balance on your accounts to score high marks here. Less is better but owing a little bit can be better than owing nothing at all because lenders want to see that you are responsible and financially stable enough to pay it back if you borrow money.

**3. *Length of Credit History: 15%***
Your credit score also considers how long you have been using credit. For how many years have you had obligations? How old is your oldest account, and what is the average age of all your accounts?

Long <u>credit history</u> is helpful (if late payments and other harmful items do not mar it), but a short history can be satisfactory too, as long as you've made your payments on time and don't owe too much.

**4. *New Credit: 10%***
Your FICO score considers how many new accounts you have. It looks at how many new accounts you have applied for recently and when the last time you opened a new account was.

Whenever you apply for a new line of credit, lenders typically make a <u>hard inquiry</u> (also called a hard pull), which is the process of checking your credit information during the underwriting procedure. This is different from a <u>soft inquiry</u>, like retrieving your credit information.

**5. *Types of Credit in Use: 10%***

The FICO formula's final thing in determining your credit score is whether you have a mix of different credit types, such as credit cards, store accounts, <u>installment loans</u>, and mortgages. It also looks at how many total accounts you have. Since this is a small component of your score, do not worry if you do not have accounts in each of these categories, and do not open new accounts to increase your mix of credit types.

When it comes to laws to protect the consumer, the <u>Federal Trade Commission (FTC)</u> and the <u>Consumer Financial Protection Bureau (CFPB)</u> are the two federal agencies charged with overseeing and enforcing the act's provisions. Many states also have laws relating to credit reporting.

The key takeaways for the Fair Credit Report Act or FCRA are

- The Fair Credit Reporting Act (FCRA) governs how credit bureaus can collect and share individual consumers' information.
- FCRA also gives consumers certain rights, including free access to their credit reports.

It offers consumer protection when it comes to their credit scores and profiles

Did you know?

Your business credit profile and scores are available to anyone who wants them. In the consumer world, someone needs your permission to pull your consumer reports. This is what the FCRA calls "permissible purpose." But with no FCRA in the business world, anyone who wants your reports can quickly and cheaply get them. This includes competitors, prospects, clients, lenders, and more.

# CHAPTER 7

## EXCLUSIVE PROGRAM TO START NOW

The sheer fact that you are reading this book lets me know you are serious about building your business credit for now and the future of your business. You are now qualified to participate in an 'Exclusive Program' only available to BCW's clients. ***The Business credit works online course & book exclusive program*** gives you very practical resources, action steps and key companies to help you get started, today.

We have selected five trade accounts choose from to get you started with today. Remember, you must apply with three trade accounts, so you have more than enough to choose from with these.

***Here is a quick review on trade accounts.*** A trade account (sometimes referred to as a vendor account) is typically a store account. As you set up your accounts with various vendors, make sure you are working towards setting up net terms. Payments on net terms are reported to the business credit bureaus.

When applying for trade accounts, make sure you use your correct business information as it matches all your business records.

Also, to ensure that all your vendors report, make sure your purchase is over $50. It typically takes 30-90 days to complete this step, and your payments to report on your business credit reports. Continue to search your reports regularly, so you are aware when they start reporting.

## Tier 1 – Apply for Vendor Accounts

**Phone:** 800-295-5510
**Website:** https://www.uline.com
**Reports to:** D&B and Experian

**Description:** Uline is the leading distributor of Shipping, Industrial, and Packing materials, Industrial and Janitorial Products. 99.5% of Uline's orders ship the same day, with no backorders.

**To Qualify:**
– Entity in good standing with Secretary of State
– EIN with IRS
– Business address- matching everywhere.
– D&B number
– Business License- if applicable
– Business Bank account
– Business Phone Number Listed in 411
– Application may be approved for a net 30 at the time of order. Upon final review, Credit Department may change to a few pre-paid orders before a Net 30 is granted

**To Apply:** We will need to create an account first, then place an order and select Net 30 terms. The Credit Department will review the account.

**Terms:** Net 30

**Phone:** 800-395-0812 option 3
**Website:** https://www.wexinc.com/solutions/fleet-management/
**Reports to:** D&B and Experian

**Description:** Wrights Express (WEX Card) offers universal fleet cards, heavy truck cards, and universally accepted business fleet cards designed with features that support the small business, including a rewards program.

**Special Instruction:** Please keep in mind, before applying for multiple accounts with WEX Fleet cards, and please make sure to have enough time in between applying so that they do not red-flagged your account for fraud.

**To Qualify:**

WEX Fleet Card (Net 15)
– Entity in good standing with Secretary of State
– EIN with IRS
– Business address- matching everywhere.
– D&B number
– Business License- if applicable
– Business Bank account
– Business Phone Number Listed in 411
– SSN is required for informational purposes. If concerned, they will pull your personal credit, and please talk to their credit department before applying.
– If not approved based on business credit history or been in business less than one year, then a $500 deposit is needed or a Personal Guarantee (PG.)

WEX Flex Card (Net 22 or Revolving)
– Entity in good standing with Secretary of State
– EIN with IRS
– Business address- matching everywhere.
– D&B number
– Business License- if applicable
– Business Bank account
– Business Phone Number Listed in 411
– No minimum time in business
– A Personal Guarantee (PG) is required

**To Apply:** Online or Over the phone

**Terms:** Net 15 (WEX Fleet Card), Net 22, or Revolving (WEX Flex Card)

**Phone:** 800-288-2000
**Website:** https://www.ebarnett.com
**Reports to:** Experian

**Description:** Home Depot Pro, formerly Barnett, powers pros to get more done. We are your single-source supplier for everything from plumbing supplies and PPE to hardware, electrical, and HVAC supplies.

**Special Note:** Barnett, Hardware Express, Supply Works, and Wilmar are one entity, each offering various products. Please only apply for one of these four accounts.

Unfortunately, virtual addresses are not accepted.

**To Qualify:**
– Entity in good standing with Secretary of State
– EIN number with IRS
– Business address- matching everywhere
– D & B number
– Business License- if applicable
– Business Bank account
– May ask to pay upfront for first purchase or two for net 30
– Virtual addresses are not accepted

**To Apply:** Online or over the phone

**Terms:** Net 30

**Phone:** 800-798-8809
**Website:** http://www.hdsupply.com/
**Reports to:** Equifax

**Description:** Has a vast selection of tools and materials. It ranges from hand tools, power tools, concrete products and accessories, rebar fabrication, fasteners, connectors, erosion control materials, pipes and fittings, waterproofing needs, drywall accessories, and everything to keep your crews safe. You will also find tool repair service or rental forms, braces, hardware, and decorative stamps at many locations.

**To Qualify:**
– Entity in good standing with Secretary of State
– EIN number with IRS
– Business address- matching everywhere.
– D&B number
– Business License- if applicable
– Business Bank account
– Bank reference
– At least 1 year in credit reporting

**To Apply:** Online

**Terms:** Net 30

**Phone:** 800-472-4643
**Website:** https://www.grainger.com/
**Reports to:** D&B

**Description:** Grainger works with more than 1,300 suppliers to provide customers with electrical, fasteners, fleet maintenance, HVACR, hardware, janitorial, material handling, pneumatics, power tools, pumps, and much more.

**To Qualify:**
– Entity in good standing with Secretary of State
– EIN with IRS
– Business address- matching everywhere.
– D&B number
– Business License- if applicable
– Business Bank account
– Business registered to Secretary of State (SOS) for at least 60 days old.
– If a business doesn't have established credit, they will require additional documents like accounts payable, income statement, balance sheets, etc.

**Apply:** Online or over the phone

**Terms:** Net 30, Net 45, Net 60, or Net 90

**TIER 2 Let us go!**

If you have gotten this far, then you have completed the first tier. Excellent job! Now it is time to move on to Tier 2. At Tier 3, you will need to have at least six trade accounts reporting on our business credit report to move forward. This is a list of next level of trade accounts that you can apply for to begin reporting.

Since you currently have at least three trade accounts reporting, now it is time to establish your business credit reports further. Please select and apply for three more trade accounts.

Remember to use your correct business information when applying, as all information should match your business records perfectly.

When you make a purchase, do so on your net /credit terms. It is payments on net/credit terms that are reported.

It takes 30-90 days from the day you make your payment for your trade account to report on your business credit report.

Here is our list of resources.

**Phone:** 866-333-9731
**Website:** https://www.uhaul.com/
**Reports to:** D&B

**Description:** U-Haul is an American moving equipment and storage rental company based in Phoenix, Arizona, in operation since 1945. Since 1945, U-Haul has been serving do-it-yourself movers and their households.

**To Qualify:**
– Entity in good standing with Secretary of State
– Business credit history
– EIN with IRS
– Business address- matching everywhere.
– D&B Number
– Business License- if applicable
– Business Bank account
– At least four years in business
– Must have an excellent D&B paydex score of 80 or higher

**To Apply:** Online

**Terms:** Net 30

**Phone:** 800-767-1358

**Website:** https://business.officedepot.com
**Reports to:** D&B, Experian, and Equifax

**Description:** Office Depot® OfficeMax® is a resource and a catalyst to help customers work better. We are a single source for everything customers need to be more productive, including the latest technology, core office supplies, print and document services, business services, facilities products, furniture, and school essentials.

**To Qualify:**

Business Account with Full Balance Due Terms (Net 30 )
– Entity in good standing with Secretary of State
– EIN with IRS
– Business address- matching everywhere.
– D&B number
– Business License- if applicable
– Business Bank account
– At least three years in business
– Must have an excellent D&B paydex score of 80 or higher
– If the above criteria are not met, a Personal Guarantee (PG is required.

Business Credit Account (Revolving)
– Entity in good standing with Secretary of State
– EIN with IRS
– Business address- matching everywhere.
– D&B number
– Business License- if applicable

– Business Bank account
– A corporation with more than $5 million annual sales and in business for at least three years
– If the above criteria are not met, a Personal Guarantee (PG is required.

**To Apply:** Online, over the phone, or at the store

**Terms:** Net 30 or Revolving

## QuikTrip

**Phone:** 888-737-7633
**Website:** https://www.quiktripfleetoffers.com/
**Reports to:** D&B and Experian

**Description:** QuikTrip provides a quick fix for those on the go. QuikTrip (QT) owns and operates about 670 gasoline/convenience stores in a dozen states, mainly in the central US QT stores, which average 4,600 sq. ft., feature the company's own QT brand of gas and diesel fuel, as well as brand-name beverages, candy, and tobacco. QT's 15-plus travel centers offer scales, food, fuel, showers, and other services for truckers. The firm's FleetMaster program offers commercial trucking companies detailed reports showing drivers' product purchases, amounts spent, and odometer readings.

**Special Instruction:** Please keep in mind, before applying for multiple accounts with WEX Fleet cards, and please make sure to have enough time in between applying so that they do not red-flagged your account for fraud.

**To Qualify:**

QT Fleetmaster
– Entity in good standing with Secretary of State
– EIN with IRS
– Business address- matching everywhere.
– D&B number
– Business License- if applicable
– Business Bank account
– Business Phone Number Listed in 411
– Gross annual revenue
– If not approved based on business credit history or been in business for less than one year, then a $500 deposit is needed or a Personal Guarantee(PG.)
– No setup, annual or monthly card fees

QT Fleetmaster Plus
– Entity in good standing with Secretary of State
– EIN with IRS
– Business address- matching everywhere.
– D&B number
– Business License- if applicable
– Business Bank account
– Business Phone Number Listed in 411
– Gross annual revenue
– If not approved based on business credit history or been in business for less than one year, then a $500

deposit is needed or a Personal Guarantee(PG.)
– There is a $40 setup fee for the account and a $2/per month/per card fee.

**To Apply:** Online or over the phone

**Terms:** Net 15

**Phone:** 800-637-1462
**Website:** https://www.valvoline.com
**Reports to:** D&B and Experian

**Description:** Quick, easy, and trusted fleet maintenance by Valvoline instant oil change. Use for care only at Valvoline Instant Oil Change locations. Use for fuel at 90% of fueling locations nationwide—anywhere the WEX® card is accepted

**Special Instruction:** Please keep in mind, before applying for multiple accounts with WEX Fleet cards, and please make sure to have enough time in between applying so that they do not red-flagged your account for fraud.

**To Qualify:**

– Entity in good standing with Secretary of State
– EIN with IRS
– Business address- matching everywhere.

– D&B number
– Business License- if applicable
– Business Bank account
– Business Phone Number Listed in 411
– SSN is required for informational purposes. If concerned, they will pull your personal credit, and please talk to their credit department before applying.
– Trade References
– If not approved based on business credit history or been in business for less than one year, then a $500 deposit is needed or a Personal Guarantee (PG.)

**To Apply:** Online or over the phone

**Terms:** Net 15

## amazon

**Phone:** 866-634-8381
**Website:** https://www.amazon.com
**Reports to:** D&B and Equifax

**Description:** Online shopping from the earth's most extensive selection of books, magazines, music, DVDs, videos, electronics, computers, software, apparel & accessories, shoes, and much more.

**To Qualify:**
– Entity in good standing with Secretary of State
– EIN with IRS

– Business address- matching everywhere.
– D&B number
– Business License- if applicable
– Business Bank account
– Business Phone Number Listed in 411
– No minimum time in business if solid business credit history
– Will pull business credit reports to make sure some established business credit history.
– Must have an excellent D&B paydex score of 80 or higher and a good Equifax business credit score
– The company has been in business for more than two years but does not have an established business credit history. A Personal Guarantee (PG) is recommended but not required. It may increase the likelihood of approval and is recommended if you have a young or small business. And not enough business credit history.

**To Apply:** Online

**Terms:** Net 55

**Phone:** 866-910-7991
**Website:** https://www.7-eleven.com/
**Reports to:** D&B and Experian

**Description:** The more you fuel at 7-Eleven, the more you save — up to 7¢ off per gallon on any fuel brand at our pumps!

**Special Instruction:** Please keep in mind, before applying for multiple accounts with WEX Fleet cards, and please make sure to have enough time in between applying so that they do not red-flagged your account for fraud.

**To Qualify:**
– Entity in good standing with Secretary of State
– EIN with IRS
– Business address- matching everywhere.
– D&B number
– Business License- if applicable
– Business Bank account
– Business Phone Number Listed in 411
– SSN is required for informational purposes. If concerned, they will pull your personal credit, and please talk to their credit department before applying.
– If not approved based on business credit history or been in business less than one year, then a $500 deposit is needed or a Personal Guarantee (PG.)

**To Apply:** Online or over the phone

**Terms:** Net 15

## TIER 3 You have the hang of it now!

You currently have at least six trade accounts reporting, but now it is time to establish your business credit reports further. Please select and apply for four more trade accounts.

Remember to use your correct business information when applying, as all information should match your business records perfectly.

When you make a purchase, do so on your net /credit terms. It is payments on net/credit terms that are reported.

To ensure that your vendors report your payments, purchase $50 or more.

On average, it takes 30-90 days for your trade accounts to report and to complete this step.

### CROWN OFFICE SUPPLIES

**Phone:** 307-317-7018
**Website:** http://crownofficesupplies.com/
**Reports to:** D&B, Experian, Equifax and CreditSafe

**Description:** Offers a variety of Office Supplies and takes helping clients seriously. The state is just starting your business, or have an existing business, but you have a question regarding office supplies...we are here to help!

**Special Instruction:** Special Instructions: There is a 99.00 annual fee, though they report that fee to the business credit bureaus. (This must be paid before you can access your tradeline). For other purchases to report needs to be a minimum of 30.00 buys.

If the order is less than $30 plus the shipping fee, it will still be reported for as long the total amount is $30 or more.

Helpful Video: https://crownofficesupplies.com/faq/

**To Qualify:**
– Entity in good standing with Secretary of State
– EIN with IRS
– Business address- matching everywhere.
– D&B number
– Business License- if applicable
– Business Bank account
– Business must be at least 90 days old.
– Has other approved vendors with a credit limit of $800 or higher.
– Membership fee is $99 annually upon approval.

**To Apply:** Online

**Terms:** Net 30

**Phone:** 818-476-7892
**Website:** https://summaofficesupplies.com/apply
**Reports to:** Tier 1 account reports to Equifax,
Tier 2 account reports to D&B

**Description:** Summa Office Supplies is the ultimate source for all your office product needs. We specialize in quality office products and supplies at guaranteed savings. We are ready to provide you and your team with the quality office supply products that are essential to your office environment.

**Special Note:** Their Tier 1 account only has limited options of products but can be gotten with limited qualifications.

Their Tier 2 account offers their complete list of products but might ask for a PG; please make sure to read their complete information listed.

**To Qualify:**
– Offer Net 30 with regular Biz foundation- $2000 limit
– Min $75.00 purchase for the first order only to report
– Entity in good standing with Secretary of State
– EIN with IRS
– Business address- matching everywhere.

– D&B number
– Business License- if applicable
– Business Bank account
– You may qualify for Tier 1 account if new in business and not enough business credit history with a minimum order of $80 of downloadable products
– You may qualify for Tier 2 account if the business has six months or more of credit reporting with a minimum order of $300 worth of office supplies upon checkout.

**To Apply:** Online

**Terms:**

Tier 1- Net 30 or Revolving (for downloadable products only)

Tier 2- Net 30 or Revolving (for both office supplies and downloadable products)

**Phone:** 708-719-4238
**Website:** https://businesstshirtclub.com/
**Reports to:** Equifax

**Description:** Business T-Shirt Club is a wholesale t-shirt and apparel buying club exclusively for business owners & entrepreneurs. Membership grants you access to premium apparel brands at wholesale rates for all your apparel needs!

**To Qualify:**
– Entity in good standing with Secretary of State
– EIN with IRS
– Business address- matching everywhere.
– D&B number
– Business License- if applicable
– Business Bank account
– Minimum order quantity for custom printed apparel is 12 items per design. For blank apparel orders, there is a minimum order amount of $250 required.
– Annual Membership- $69.99

**To Apply:** Online

**Terms:** Net 30

**Phone:** 866-325-6961
**Website:** https://www.stripesfleetcards.com/
**Reports to**: D&B and Experian

**Description:** The Stripes fleet card program is designed to help businesses optimize savings, receive competitive fuel rebates at Stripes Stores, and fuel almost anywhere in the US.

**Special Instruction:** Please keep in mind, before applying for multiple accounts with WEX Fleet cards, and please make sure to have enough time in between applying so that they do not red-flagged your account for fraud.

**To Qualify:**
– Entity in good standing with Secretary of State
– EIN with IRS
– Business address- matching everywhere.
– D&B number
– Business License- if applicable
– Business Bank account
– Business Phone Number Listed in 411
– SSN is required for informational purposes. If concerned, they will pull your personal credit, and please talk to their credit department before applying.
– If not approved based on business credit history or been in business less than one year, then a $500 deposit is needed or a Personal Guarantee (PG.)

**To Apply:** Online or over the phone

**Terms:** Net 15

**Phone:** 888-260-0886
**Website:** https://www.shell.us

**Reports to:** D&B and Experian

**Description:** Shell is a global group of energy and petrochemical companies. A Shell Card will help you keep vehicles in shape and your expenses under control.

**Special Instruction:** Please keep in mind, before applying for multiple accounts with WEX Fleet cards, and please make sure to have enough time in between applying so that they do not red-flagged your account for fraud.

**To Qualify:**

Shell Fleet Navigator® and Shell Fleet Plus®
– Entity in good standing with Secretary of State
– EIN with IRS
– Business address- matching everywhere.
– D&B number
– Business License- if applicable
– Business Bank account
– Business Phone Number Listed in 411
– SSN is required for informational purposes. If concerned, they will pull your personal credit, and please talk to their credit department before applying.
– If not approved based on business credit history or been in business less than one year, then a $500 deposit is needed or a Personal Guarantee (PG.)

Shell Small Business Mastercard™
– Entity in good standing with Secretary of State
– EIN with IRS
– Business address- matching everywhere.
– D&B number

– Business License- if applicable
– Business Bank account
– Business Phone Number Listed in 411
– No minimum time in business
– A Personal Guarantee (PG) is required

**To Apply:** Online or over the phone

**Terms:** Net 15

**Phone:** 800-633-3271
**Website:** https://www.fleetcardsusa.com
**Reports:** D&B, Experian, and Equifax

**Description:** The ARCO Business Solutions program provides more features, benefits, and controls for every driver in your fleet. Their Business Solutions Fuel Card provides fleet managers with detailed reporting and individual spending controls. You are accepted at over 1,500 participating ARCO locations in the United States. ARCO Business Solutions Mastercard® gives your drivers the flexibility of fueling at ARCO locations and any other fuel location in the United States where Mastercard is accepted. Experience complete online control 24/7.

**Special Instructions:** The first payment made to Arco when you have a Net account can take up to 90 days to report. After that, it reports monthly.

**To Qualify:**

Arco Business Solutions Fuel Card
– Entity in good standing with Secretary of State
– EIN with IRS
– Business address- matching everywhere.
– D&B number
– Business License- if applicable
– Business Bank account
– Business Phone Number Listed in 411
– In business for at least one year
– Can only be used at Arco locations.
– If not enough business credit history, may ask for a Personal Guarantee (PG.)

Arco Business Solutions Mastercard
– Entity in good standing with Secretary of State
– EIN with IRS
– Business address- matching everywhere.
– D&B number
– Business License- if applicable
– Business Bank account
– Business Phone Number Listed in 411
– Can be used to gas stations outside of Arco.
– If not enough business credit history, may ask for a Personal Guarantee (PG.)

**To Apply:** Online or over the phone

**Terms:** Net 7, Net 10, or Net 15

**Tier four- Congratulations!**

You have made it to the 4$^{th}$ and final tier. Apply for 4 trade accounts.

You currently have at least ten trade accounts reporting, but now it is time to establish your business credit reports further. Please select and apply for four more trade accounts.

Remember to use your correct business information when applying, as all information should match your business records perfectly.

When you make a purchase, do so on your net /credit terms. It is payments on net/credit terms that are reported.

To ensure that your vendors report your payments, purchase $50 or more. Need help? Call our advisor team for details.

On average, it takes 30-90 days for your trade accounts to report and to complete this step.

Commerce Bank

**Phone:** 800-892-7104 option 2
**Website:** https://www.commercebank.com/
**Reports to:** D&B and Experian

**Description:** At Commerce Bank, we have over 150 years of experience and many strong, established products to back us up. From Bloomington, Illinois to Denver, Colorado, and at 184 branches in between, we serve individuals, families, businesses and communities at the local branch, the ATM, online and through our 24/7 customer service line. Commerce Bank serves customers in Missouri, Kansas, Illinois, Oklahoma, and Colorado.

**To Qualify:**
– Entity in good standing with Secretary of State
– Business credit history
– EIN number with IRS
– Business address- matching everywhere.
– D&B number
– Business License- if applicable
– Business Bank account
– No minimum time in business
– Must have at least $5M in annual revenue
– If less than $5M in annual revenue, a Personal Guarantee (PG) is required.
– For-profit businesses with annual revenue of $5 million or greater may choose to be underwritten based on company liability, provided that financial statements and a Corporate Resolution are also submitted.
– Any business within Commerce Bank's retail lending area (MO, KS, IL, OK, CO) only can apply.
– Cash advance available with business credit card approval, amount of cash advance depends upon approval amount.

**To Apply:** At a branch if online they may require a PG.

**Terms:** Net 30 or Revolving

**Phone:** 800-633-3271
**Website:** https://www.universalpremiumcard.com/
**Reports to:** D&B and Experian

**Description:** Universal Fleet Mastercard help prevent fraud, monitor spending, and track where your drivers purchase fuel. Businesses like yours need to manage fuel expenses but cannot be tied down to fueling only in a limited network. The Universal Premium Mastercard® lets you control fuel spending everywhere Mastercard if accepted so you can keep your business running smoothly.

**To Qualify**

– Entity in good standing with Secretary of State
– EIN number with IRS
– Business address- matching everywhere.
– D&B number
– Business License- if applicable
– Business Bank account
– 10 Trade accounts reporting
– At least 3 years in business
– Must have 6 or more employees
– If not enough business credit history or is new in

businessman Personal Guarantee (PG) or a deposit can be made.
– If the above criteria are met, they will still ask for SSN on the application but used only to verify your credit and will not be shared with any third parties.

**To Apply:** Online or over the phone

**Terms:** Net 7, Net 10, Net 15 or Revolving

## SAMS CLUB

**Phone:** 800-362-6196
**Website:** https://www.samsclub.com/sams/homepage.jsp
**Reports to:** D&B

**Description:** Sam's Club is a warehouse retail chain offering office supplies, business furniture, vending items, janitorial/cleaning supplies, paper products, food service supplies, computers, and more.

**To Qualify:**

– Entity in good standing with Secretary of State
– EIN with IRS
– Business address- matching everywhere.
– D&B number
– Business License- if applicable

– Business Bank account
– Business Phone Number Listed in 411
– Must have Club membership

As stated on their application, if less than the below items might be harder to be approved without a Personal Guarantee (PG) but can try:

– $5 million in annual sales or revenues
– At least two years in business
– More than ten employees
– A Personal Guarantee (PG) is required if a company is a Sole Proprietor or Partnership
– Cash advance available with business credit card approval. The amount of cash advance depends upon the approval amount.

**To Apply:** At the store
**Terms:** Revolving
**Phone:** 888-531-3717

**Website:** https://www.chevron.com
**Reports to:** D&B and Experian

**Description:** Chevron / Texaco Universal Business Card gives you a turn-key system to help control and monitor fuel expenses. The Business Card is accepted at thousands of Chevron and Texaco stations for gasoline, tires, batteries, and more.

**Special Instruction:** Please keep in mind, before applying for multiple accounts with WEX Fleet cards, and please make sure to have enough time in between applying so that they do not red-flagged your account for fraud.

**To Qualify:**
– Entity in good standing with Secretary of State
– EIN with IRS
– Business address- matching everywhere.
– D&B number
– Business License- if applicable
– Business Bank account
– Business Phone Number Listed in 411
– SSN is required for informational purposes. If concerned, they will pull your personal credit, and please talk to their credit department before applying.
– Established business credit
– Prefers in Business for over 18 months.
– If not approved based on business credit history or been in business for less than 1 1/2 years, then a $500 deposit is needed or a Personal Guarantee (PG.)

**To Apply:** Online or over the phone
**Terms:** Net 7

**Phone:** 855-854-2688
**Website:** https://www.americanexpress.com/us/credit-cards/business/corporate-credit-cards/?inav=footer_corp_prg
**Reports to:** D&B

**Description:** American Express offers world-class Charge and Credit Cards, Gift Cards, Rewards, Travel, Personal Savings, Business Services, Insurance, and more.

**To Qualify:**
AMEX Corporate Start-up Account
– Entity in good standing with Secretary of State
– EIN with IRS
– Business address- matching everywhere.
– D & B number
– Business License- if applicable
– Business Bank account
– Bank statement for the last three months, with a minimum of $1-2 million bank account balance.
AMEX Corporate Account
– Entity in good standing with Secretary of State
– EIN with IRS
– Business address- matching everywhere.
– D & B number
– Business License- if applicable
– Business Bank account

– Has a minimum of $4M in annual revenue
– At least two years of financial statement

**To Apply:** Online or over the phone

**Terms:** Net 30

**Website:** https://www.ally.com
**Reports to:** D&B, Experian, and Equifax

**Description:** Ally offers commercial vehicle financing. It gives personal funding but also reports to business credit bureaus. If your business qualifies for financing without the owner's guaranty, you can obtain financing in the business name only. This gives you the ability to save your credit for other use as well.

**To Qualify:**

– Entity in good standing with Secretary of State
– EIN with IRS
– Business address- matching everywhere.
– D&B number
– Business License- if applicable
– Business Bank account
– Bank reference
– Fleet financing references
– Apply in business only. The dealer will advise if an approved, or Personal Guarantee (PG) needed

– If PG is used, will not report on personal bureaus unless the account defaults

**To Apply:** At Dealership only. Dealer locations are listed on their website.

**Terms:** Lease or Loan

**Phone:** 866-462-5035

**Website:** https://www.circlek.com
**Reports to:** D&B and Experian

**Description:** Circle K offers a private labeled fleet card. With the Circle K Fleet Card, you can save up to 4¢ a gallon (based on monthly gallons purchased at Circle K locations).

**Special Instruction:** Please keep in mind, before applying for multiple accounts with WEX Fleet cards, and please make sure to have enough time in between applying so that they do not red-flagged your account for fraud.

**To Qualify:**

– Entity in good standing with Secretary of State
– EIN with IRS
– Business address- matching everywhere.
– D&B number

– Business License- if applicable
– Business Bank account
– Business Phone Number Listed in 411
– SSN is required for informational purposes. If concerned, they will pull your personal credit please talk to their credit department before applying.
– If not approved based on business credit history or been in business less than one year, then a $500 deposit is needed or a Personal Guarantee (PG)

**To Apply:** Online or over the phone at 888-626-1218

**Terms:** Net 15

**Phone:** 844-725-9569
**Website:** https://brex.com/
**Reports to:** D&B and Experian

**Description:** Brex is rebuilding B2B financial products, starting with a corporate card for technology companies. We help startups of all sizes (from recently incorporated to later-stage companies) to get a card that has 20x higher limits instantly, completely automates expense management, kills receipt tracking, and magically integrates with their accounting systems.

**Special Instruction:** They offer two types of business credit account- for Start-up businesses and E-commerce. They do not offer balance transfers from other credit cards to Brex due to non-PG. They do balance transfers within Brex credit accounts only. They offer points that can be redeemed towards payment credit. Use Brex points to purchase hotels and flights through their internal travel portal or transfer Brex points towards air miles to participating airlines.

**To Qualify:**

– Entity in good standing with Secretary of State
– EIN with IRS
– Business address- matching everywhere.
– D&B number
– Business License- if applicable
– Business Bank account
– No Personal Guarantee is required.

– For Start-Up Account:
– No minimum time in business
– Average bank balance of $100,000 to get approved for Net 30
– Average bank balance of $50,000 and below with Professional Investors like Venture Capital and Private Equity.

**To Apply:** Online

**Terms – Net** 30

# TOYOTA

**Phone:** 800-331-4331
**Website:** https://www.toyota.com/
**Reports to:** Experian and Equifax

**Description:** Toyota Motor Corporation is a global automotive industry leader manufacturing vehicles in 27 countries or regions and marketing its products in over 170 countries and territories. Founded in 1937 and headquartered in Toyota City, Japan, Toyota Motor Corporation employs nearly 350,000 people globally.

**To Qualify:**
– Entity in good standing with Secretary of State
– EIN with IRS
– Business address- matching everywhere.
– D&B number
– Business License- if applicable
– Business Bank account
– Bank reference
– Trade/credit references
– Good business credit history
– At least two years in business
– If not approved based on business credit history or been in business less than two years, then a Personal Guarantee(PG) is required.

**To Apply:** At the Dealership – https://www.toyota.com/dealers/

**Terms:** Revolving

It is a done deal. Congratulations is in order! You have completed all 4 Rounds. What does this mean?

- You have formed a solid business foundation
- Established your business credit reports
- Learned to monitor and read your business credit reports
- Built business credit and more

Remember, continue to build your business credit & look for additional learning or advanced tactics to take your business credit to the next level.

I want to take this time to thank everyone who read this book and took action. You should be commending yourself. I am commending you because you have really changed the trajectory of your business for the better. In my book, no pun intended, that is noteworthy.

When you started your business, it was one big idea, your obsession. You did whatever it took to live your dreams. Your dream, not anyone else's and you did that.

You invested your time and your hard-earned money. You took out $2^{nd}$ mortgages, priceless goods were sold just to keep the lights on. Friendships were lost. Sacrifices were made, you hired coaches and mentors. You sought out every guru under the sun to help your business be successful.

Why? Well, it is because you know you have a winner. It is your company. It is your baby. You love it and want to see it successful. But there is a huge problem standing in your way. Cash, Credit and Financing are the components of the problem. I know. It is tough getting the cash and credit you need to open, grow, and expand your business.

So, what do you do? You use your personal credit, cash, and personal assets. The downside is that's risky business. It is precarious to put your family, personal credit, and personal assets in jeopardy. There is no need for that. Real, solid, and true help is here and just what our business credit needs.

My name is Darryl Johnson, and I am the founder of Business Credit works. I am on a mission to educate, explain and empower business owners with a better way to structure their business.

*Stop us if any of this sounds familiar…*

- You have been over-extending your credit to keep your business afloat, and your scores have taken a hit.
- Your credit is less-than-stellar, and you have been paying out of pocket for all business expenses.
- You signed up for another business credit building program in the past and got nothing but a to-do list with no real help.
- You have been trying to build business credit with old forum information and outdated DIY programs, but you have not gotten anywhere.

# ABOUT THE AUTHOR

Darryl Johnson, Business Credit Works Founder & Financial Consultant

After 20 years in corporate America, Darryl is pursuing his passion of helping other entrepreneurs access the capital they need to achieve their dreams. He has previously worked with:

Wells Fargo
BNY Wealth Management Bank
Bank of America
Pennymac Loan Servicing
J.P. Morgan Chase
Desert Schools Federal Credit Union
Alliance Financial Services
Charles Schwab Brokerage

Utilizing his experience in lending and finance, Darryl started Business Credit Works, rather than using a cookie-cutter approach to business credit; Business Credit Works take a customized approach as we believe every business is unique with unique needs, funding goals, and credit demands. Our mission has never changed: We will help you build a creditworthy business and obtain the funding you need without having to put your personal credit or personal assets at risk every time.

Darryl currently serves as the Business Commissioner for the first KC LGBTQ Commission. and as a board member on the Black Excellence KC (BXKC).

www.ingramcontent.com/pod-product-compliance
Lightning Source LLC
Chambersburg PA
CBHW050246220526
45465CB00002B/565